CARD TRICKS

STERLING INNOVATION

New York

STERLING INNOVATION
New York

An Imprint of Sterling Publishing Co., Inc.
1166 Avenue of the Americas
New York, NY 10036

This publication is a component of the *Card Tricks* kit (ISBN: 978-1-4351-6898-5)
and is not to be sold separately.

Distributed in Canada by Sterling Publishing Co., Inc.
c/o Canadian Manda Group, 664 Annette Street
Toronto, Ontario M6S 2C8, Canada

For information about custom editions, special sales, and premium and corporate purchases,
please contact Sterling Special Sales at 800-805-5489 or specialsales@sterlingpublishing.com.

Manufactured in China

2 4 6 8 10 9 7 5 3 1

sterlingpublishing.com

Interior design by Ian Midson
Photography by Amanda Heywood

Contents

Introduction

All the tricks in this book are easy to learn and simple to perform. Even so, a little time spent in rehearsal will enhance their impact and improve your reputation as a performer.

So how much practice does a card trick require? Enough to ensure that you perform it smoothly and can handle the cards with confidence. No one believes in a performer who is nervous or who is not in control of the material. Practice until a trick becomes second nature, and you will give your presentation the polish these fine tricks deserve.

It is also a good idea to memorize the two golden rules of magical performance. Rule One: Never do the same trick twice for the same audience, no matter how hard they plead with you. Rule Two: Never bore your audience. Stop performing while they still want to see more. That way, you will be asked to entertain them another time.

Above all else, enjoy your magic. Card tricks are designed to divert and entertain, and there is no reason why you shouldn't enjoy each performance as much as your audience does.

SELF-WORKING TRICKS

ALL YOU HAVE TO DO TO PERFORM THE TRICKS IN THIS

SECTION IS TO FOLLOW THE INSTRUCTIONS AND LEARN THE

SIMPLE STEPS. EVERYTHING IS AUTOMATIC, ALTHOUGH

A LITTLE TIME SPENT POLISHING YOUR

PRESENTATION WON'T HURT.

DO AS I DO

The Effect

Performer and spectator have a deck of cards each, which they shuffle. Each then makes a selection from his or her own deck. Astonishingly, they choose identical cards.

The Method

Use a red-backed and a blue-backed deck, so they can be easily distinguished. Give one deck to a spectator, saying, "Whatever I do, you do the same."

The decks are shuffled and cut, then you and the spectator exchange decks. Shuffle as before, then exchange decks again, returning the spectator's deck face down; do this by holding the deck with your fingers at one end, thumb at the other, and move it past your line of vision as you lay it down.

As you glimpse the bottom card (e.g. the Four of Diamonds), remember it (**Fig. 1**).

"Do as I do . . .," you say. Then spread your own deck in a ribbon (a long arc or line), lift a card from the middle of the spread and look at it (**Fig. 2**).

Now say, "Take a card and remember it." In fact, you simply go through the motions. There is no need to remember your card.

Square the face-down deck and put the chosen card on top, face down. The spectator does the same. Now make a complete cut, burying the chosen card.

"Give me your deck again, and you take mine."

Swap decks and tell the spectator to take the card he or she looked at from your deck and put it face down on the table. Then say, "And I'll take mine from your deck."

Spread the cards, faces towards you, looking for the remembered Four of Diamonds. When you find it, the card underneath will be the spectator's chosen card.

Remove it and put it face down in front of you (**Fig. 3**).

"Show us your card," you say.

The spectator turns over his or her card. Then turn your card. They are both the same.

"Well, you certainly did what I did!"

TURN-OVER CARD MYSTERY

The Effect

A spectator takes a card from the deck and remembers it. It is put back, and when the deck is spread, the chosen card has turned face up.

The Method

Before you begin, turn the bottom card of the face-down deck face up. When you spread the cards (**Fig. 1**), make sure the bottom card doesn't show.

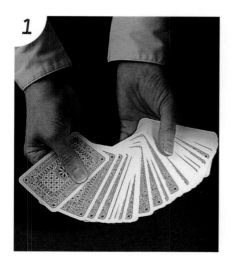

1

left hand and tell him or her to let others see it. "Tonight, I'll allow witnesses," you say.

As the card is shown around, your left hand drops casually to your side; on the way down, let the deck turn over in your hand. Do not rush this.

When you bring the hand up again, you are holding a squared-up deck with one face-down card on top. The rest are face up.

Ask the spectator to take a card, then square the deck in your

Take the chosen card from the spectator, keeping it face down, and push it very deliberately into the deck (**Fig. 2**). Square up the cards.

"If I were a beginner at this," you say, "I'd try to find your card like this . . . ."

Put the deck behind your back and look worried, like someone hopelessly fumbling for a card. In fact, you turn the top card over to face the same way as the rest, then turn over the whole deck, so it is face down. Bring the cards into view. They have been out of sight for only a moment, and everyone believes it was just a swift gag.

"But I'm a first-class operator," you say, "so I use real magic." Put the deck face down on the table and prepare to spread the cards in a long ribbon. "What was the name of your card?" you ask.

As soon as the card is named, spread the deck (**Fig. 3**) and reveal the chosen card, now amazingly face upwards in the spread.

CARD SHARP

The Effect

You mix the cards to a spectator's instructions, but they end up the same as they were at the start. The first time you do this trick it will probably fool you, too!

The Method

Take all 13 cards of one suit and lay them in numerical order on the table (**Fig.1**). Tell a spectator to note the strict order of the cards, then square up the pile and turn it face down in your left hand.

"We want to make sure the cards are thoroughly mixed," you say, "so you will tell me how to deal them."

Explain that when the spectator says "Deal," you will put a card on the table (**Fig. 2**). When he or she says "Dip," you will take the second card from the pile and put it on top of the first card (**Fig. 3**), then deal both cards together onto the table.

1

When all are dealt, pick up the pile and say:

"The truth is, whatever you tell me to do, the cards always go where I tell them to go."

Turn over the cards and spread them in a line. Sure enough, all 13 are back in numerical order, just as they were at the start.

You proceed to deal all the cards in a pile on the table, following the spectator's instructions to "Deal" or "Dip" until all the cards are dealt. Now pick up the pile and square it.

"That has upset the order of the cards," you say, "but to upset them even further, we will go through the whole thing one more time."

Once more you deal out the cards, carefully "Dealing" or "Dipping" as instructed.

X-RAY VISION

The Effect

A spectator cuts a deck of cards into three face-down piles on the table. You gaze at the cards for a moment, then one by one you correctly name the top cards in the three piles.

The Method

Before you start, you must know the name of the top card in the deck. This is not difficult; just glimpse the card as you spread the deck, casually showing that it is ordinary (**Fig. 1**).

Put the deck face down on the table and ask a spectator to cut it into three roughly equal piles, keeping the cards face down. As this is being done, you must keep track of the pile with your known card on top (**Fig. 2**). Let's say it's the Ten of Spades.

You announce that you have X-ray vision. "I've got enough to let me see through paper and other materials for about one thirty-second of an inch. That's just deep enough to read the identity of a playing card." Pause, then add, "Sometimes."

You point to one of the piles, not the one with the known card on top, frown for a second, then say, "That card is the Ten of Spades."

Pick up the card without revealing its face (**Fig. 3**), and smile as if you were right. We will assume this card is the Three of Diamonds.

Then point to the other pile with an unknown card on top and say, "That's the Three of Diamonds."

Pick up the card as before

(it's the King of Hearts, say), smile as you square it against the other card you hold, and point to the remaining pile. This one has the remembered Ten of Spades on top. "And that," you say, "is the King of Hearts." Pick up the card, smile again, and add it to the other two.

You put the cards on the table one at a time, face up, naming each one as you do (**Fig. 4**). The effect is direct and impressive. You have accurately revealed the names of three playing cards without being able to see their faces.

STOP WHEN YOU LIKE

The Effect

A spectator deals cards until he or she wants to stop. The last card dealt is turned over and revealed to be the card identified in a note to the spectator.

The Method

Before you begin, write "You will stop at the Four of Spades" on a piece of paper and place this inside a wallet. Put the wallet and the Four of Spades in your pocket.

Ask the spectator to shuffle the cards. "Now deal them," you say, "and stop when you want."

As you say this, indicate that the cards can be dropped anywhere on the table top—an overly neat pile is the last thing you want.

While the cards are being dealt, take out the wallet, with the card face down underneath it. Rehearse this so that you can do it without fumbling. When the dealing stops, drop the wallet onto the pile of

cards, thus adding the Four of Spades to the pile.

"Look inside the wallet," you say. The spectator reads the note inside. You move the wallet and turn over the top card on the pile, showing the same message.

TRICKS WITH MARKED CARDS

THE FIVE TRICKS THAT FOLLOW USE SPECIAL CARDS,

EASILY MADE, TO ENABLE YOU TO PERFORM CLOSE-UP

MAGIC THAT LOOKS PROFESSIONAL.

WHILE NO SLEIGHT-OF-HAND IS REQUIRED,

THESE ARE EFFECTS THAT CREATE THE

IMPRESSION OF ADVANCED

CARD-HANDLING SKILL.

ODD DIVISION

The Method

Cut a sheet of A4 paper into 20 or 30 squares. On all but one of them write the word "Spades." On the remaining one write "Hearts." Crumple the papers and drop them into a plastic bag; the one marked "Hearts" goes in your pocket. You also need a dice, and a Three of Spades marked as shown (**Fig. 1**). This can be done using a water-resistant felt marker with a fine point.

1

To perform, say you have a card in your pocket which you placed there as the result of a premonition. "It's the card that I knew someone would choose."

Put the card face down on the table. Introduce the bag of folded papers. (Your own piece of paper is already tucked between the tips of your index and middle fingers).

"These pieces of paper all have suits written on them," you say, reaching into the bag and apparently drawing one out. You bring out the one that was already between your fingers (**Fig. 2**). "See, this says 'Hearts.' Now somebody take one."

A spectator draws Spades. "That determines the card's suit," you say. Show the dice. "Now roll that, then add the number on top to the one on the bottom."

The spectator rolls, say, a five (**Fig. 3**). He or she adds five to the bottom number, which is two.

Now say, "Divide the total by two and that will be the number of the card."

The spectator says that comes to three and a half.

"Really? Are you sure?" you say. Then you sigh. "I thought it was weird, but who can argue with fate?"

Turn over the Three-and-a-half of Spades. The response to this mystifying trick should be gratifying. (The numbers on opposite sides of a dice, incidentally, always add up to seven.)

THE ESTIMATE

The Effect

You obtain an estimate of a card's position in the deck. The estimate seems unlikely, but it turns out to be right.

The Method

Tear a quarter off a card. Place the card under five face-down cards (**Fig. 1**). Mark the upper left corner of the top card. Conceal the cards at the bottom of the deck.

1

To perform, spread the deck, being careful to keep the bottom cards bunched together to conceal the torn card. Ask a spectator to take a card (**Fig. 2**). When he or she has done that, put the deck on the table.

Say, "Remember your card, then put it face down on top of the deck." The spectator complies. "Now give the deck a complete cut, burying your card." The chosen card will now be directly under the torn card.

2

"I'm going to find your card by sensing its vibrations," you announce, and begin to thumb through the face-down cards. When you see the card with the dot, cut it to the top so that the card and the cards beneath it move to the top (**Fig. 3**). Then square the deck. Look confident as you turn over the marked card and say, "Is this your card?" It isn't.

You sigh and say you knew all along this wasn't the card: "I just chose this one because it'll give me an estimate . . . ."

Put the card to your ear. Listen and nod slowly. Put the card on the bottom of the deck and say, "The estimate is four and three-quarters."

Count the cards aloud, from the top of the deck. As you say, "Four," put down the fourth card and lift the mutilated one. (**Fig. 4**) ". . . And, er, three-quarters."

Drop the torn card and pick up the next one. Ask the spectator to name the chosen card. Turn over the card in your hand and reveal that your earlier estimate was correct.

EDUCATED CARDS

The Effect

You take turns with a spectator at laying cards on the table. You put down a card which bears the prophetic message "You've Run Out Of Cards."

The Method

Make the message card by sticking a label across the face of another card. (**Fig. 1**). Place this card at the 21st position from the top of the face-down deck.

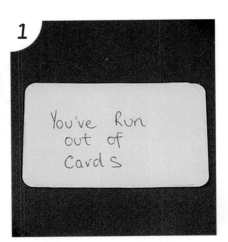

To perform, ask a spectator to cut some cards from the top of the deck, which is on the table, and put them in his or her pocket.

"Not too many," you tell the spectator, "or we'll be here all night . . . ." This ensures that fewer than 21 cards are taken! "And now I'll have some."

You must take 21 cards, and reverse their order. To do this, pick up the deck and deal 21 cards onto the table, one on top of the other (**Fig. 2**); don't make it obvious that you are counting. Put the deck aside and pick up your 21 cards.

"OK," you say, "now we'll deal cards on the table alternately. Me first."

You deal a card, turning it face up as you do, then the spectator takes one from his or her pocket and deals it (**Fig. 3**). Continue until you deal the message card. The spectator reaches in his or her pocket and finds that all the cards have gone (**Fig. 4**). As you'll discover, this trick is automatic, but it gives the impression of considerable skill on the part of the perfomer.

THE VANISHING QUEEN

The Method

Prepare a Queen of Hearts by making two windows where the hearts were (**Fig. 1**). (You may need to use a scalpel to make the cut-out holes convincing enough to fool an onlooker.)

This is your gimmick. Now lay the Fours from the deck in a face-up pile, with the Four of Hearts on top. Drop the gimmick on top. The face card looks like a Queen of Hearts. Put this set-up in your pocket.

1

To perform, bring out the cards, displaying the apparent Queen of Hearts on the top. Turn your hand over, so the backs of the cards are uppermost, and reach underneath with your forefinger. You seem to pull out the face card (supposedly the Queen of Hearts); in fact, you put your finger in the window opening of the gimmick and slide out the second card, the Four of Hearts. Put this on the table face down.

Repeat the above with the second and third "Queens," really laying Fours on the table. Be careful to hold the cards so the thumb and little finger conceal the index marks on the gimmick (**Fig. 2**).

You show the final Queen, which is really the gimmick with a Four behind. Put this pair in your pocket, letting the back of the Four stay in view. The gimmick drops down into the pocket.

"Watch this Queen," you say, pointing to the protruding card (**Fig. 3**).

"Watch these three, too," you add, indicating the cards on the table.

Now ask if anyone remembers the suit of the Queen sticking out of your pocket. Whatever the reply, pull the card out and show that it is a Four. Ask a spectator to turn over the face-down cards on the table. They are all Fours. Applause.

CHATTY JOKER

The Method

You need two identical Jokers. Cut one in half and write your message on the other. Put the Joker with the message face up on top of the deck. Put the half Joker over it and hold them together with a rubber band around the middle; thus the half Joker will be held in place and its missing bottom concealed. On the face of it, the top card is a complete Joker.

To perform, drop the deck of cards on the table, drawing attention to the Joker: "That's a very clever card," you say. "It can always get its message across."

Pick up the cards and start to pull out the Joker from under the rubber band, grasping it at the lower end—that is, you are taking out the complete Joker. As you do so, turn the packet over so that it is face down by the time you draw the Joker out. Put the Joker face down on the table. Drop the cards into your pocket. In the same move, take out your pen and lay it a short distance from the card. Tell a spectator to put one hand on the pen and the other on the card. "Now," you say, "close your eyes and count to three." Then tell the spectator to turn the card. The message will be there for all to see.

MIND-READING WITH CARDS

PLAYING CARDS HAVE ALWAYS BEEN ASSOCIATED

WITH MIND-READING. IN THIS SECTION YOU LEARN

TO PERFORM TRICKS WHICH HAVE ALL THE MYSTERY

AND APPEAL OF AUTHENTIC PARANORMAL

DEMONSTRATIONS—AND THEY ARE A LOT EASIER

THAN THEY LOOK.

IMPOSSIBLE ODDS

The Method

You will need all the black cards from the deck, plus one red card, which you place at the 13th position from the top. Do not let anyone know how your 27-card stack is made up. Put a rubber band around the cards and keep them in your pocket. You will also need to prepare a prediction (**Fig. 1**).

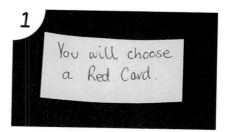

1

You will choose a Red Card.

To perform, put the folded prediction on the table. Ask a spectator to imagine a clock, and imagine it chiming an hour. He or she is to put the cards behind his or her back and count cards from the top of the pile corresponding to the hour. The spectator keeps the cards he or she has counted and hands the remaining cards back to you.

2

You now lay out the cards in the form of a clock face (**Fig. 2**), starting at the 12 o'clock position and working counterclockwise to one o'clock.

Ask the spectator what hour he or she chose. Count around to that position from the 12 o'clock card and ask the spectator to turn over the card. It will be the red card (**Fig. 3**). Ask another spectator to read out the prediction: "You will choose a red card."

Not exactly a shocking revelation. You ask the first spectator to look at the cards he or she still holds. "They're all black, aren't they?" you ask.

The spectator agrees. Now turn over the few remaining cards after you've finished making the clock face. "These are black, too, aren't they?" you ask.

Finally, one by one, you turn over the rest of the clock cards, showing that they, too, are all black (**Fig. 4**).

"There was only one red card," you say. "You chose it, and I predicted you would."

MENTAL GUIDANCE

The Effect

A spectator picks a card. Without looking, he or she pushes another card into the deck right beside his or her selection. You locate the spectator's selection. How?

The Method

Tell the spectator, "Take half the deck, give me the rest, and put your half behind your back. Now, take out any card, look at it, then put it on top of your half of the deck."

"I'll show you first," you say. Put your half behind your back; turn the second card face upwards (**Fig. 1**). Do this by lifting two cards with the right hand, pulling the second card down

with the left thumb, and flipping it over before the other card is dropped on top. This takes less than a second and should happen as the cards are being put behind your back. Now slip off the bottom card and bring it into view (**Fig. 2**) to the top; then turn the top card face up and push it in anywhere near the center (**Fig. 3**). "As you push this one in," you say, "I will send you mental guidance."

NOTE: The insertion of top and bottom cards is a red herring. It gets the spectator accustomed to the maneuver—and it brings the turned-over card to the top!

demonstrate that you have chosen a card. Put the card behind you again, but put it face up on the bottom of your deck, which you bring to the front.

"Now do as I showed you," you say. When this has been done, the spectator brings his or her cards to the front and you put yours on top. "Now your card is buried," you say.

Tell the spectator to hide the whole deck behind him or her and do this: Push the top card into the deck near the bottom; push the bottom card in near

The big finish: Spread the cards, showing there is one face up near the center, as expected (**Fig. 4**). But beneath it is the card chosen by the spectator, located through your mental guidance.

ASTOUNDING!

The Effect

You predict the identity of a card freely chosen under seemingly impossible conditions.

The Method

Any Ace and any Four must be removed from the deck and set aside. Do this openly, keeping the cards face down, explaining that they are your prediction cards.

To perform, hand the deck to a spectator to shuffle, and ask him or her to think of a number between one and 10, to be kept secret. Now tell the spectator to put the deck under the table and remove the number of cards that corresponds to his or her chosen number—i.e., if the number is four, he or she removes four cards (**Fig. 1**). The spectator must put those cards in his or her pocket and hand back the deck.

"Now I'm going to start counting the deck," you say. "When I get to the number you're thinking of, I want you to memorize it." You count the cards from the top of the deck, calling the number of each as you show its face, reversing the order as you put them down (**Fig. 2**).

Count this way until you reach number 10; count one more, saying "Eleven," then ask if the spectator has remembered his or her card. As you say this, show and deal two more cards without calling out numbers. This action is never questioned. You have dealt 13 cards in total. Put the dealt cards on top of

the deck, and almost as an after-thought hold out the deck and tell the spectator to put back the cards he or she took off (**Fig. 3**). The spectator's chosen card is 14th from the top. This is automatic. Show the Ace and Four you removed at the start.

"Fourteen," you say. "That is my prediction."

Tell the spectator to count down to the 14th card (**Fig. 4**) and put it on the table, face down. When that is done, ask for the name of his or her card. Pause, then turn over the card on the table. Astounding!

THREE TIMES RIGHT

The Effect

A number, a color, and a playing card are all successfully predicted by the performer.

The Method

This employs the one-ahead principle, used in X-Ray Vision (page 12). You need a notepad, a pen, and a deck of cards with a known card on top—say the King of Clubs.

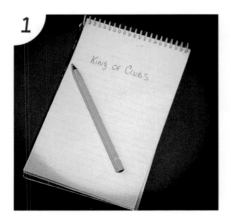

Ask a spectator to think of a color. Look pensive, then seem to be writing a color on the pad. Actually, you write, "King of Clubs," but don't let anyone see (**Fig. 1**). Tear off the sheet and fold it twice. Now ask the spectator to name the color—e.g., yellow.

To perform, tell your audience you will make a triple prediction. Produce the notepad and the pen. Put the cards on the table.

Ask another spectator to take out a dollar bill and note the last three numbers on it. On the pad write, "Yellow." Fold the paper twice and drop it next to the first one. The spectator now names the numbers—say, 246.

Tell a third spectator to cut the cards and put the cut cards beside the rest of the deck. Immediately pick up the lower half of the deck. "We'll mark the cut," you say, as you lay this part across the top of the other, making a cross shape (**Fig. 2**). The King of Clubs is now on top of the lower part of the deck.

Now you write 246. Fold the paper and drop it on top of the other two papers. Lift the top part of the deck and take off the card under the cut.

Say, "Let's see your card." Show it is the King of Clubs (**Fig. 3**).

Now pick up and open the pieces of paper. Ask the first spectator to name the chosen color; put the paper with "Yellow" written on it face up on the table. Do the same with the numbers and, for your finale, the name of the card.

PREDICTION

The Effect

Put a sealed envelope containing your prediction on the table. A spectator chooses a card, and is asked to open the envelope. Inside is a duplicate of his or her chosen card.

The Method

To prepare, put a duplicate of the "force" card (here the Eight of Hearts) in an envelope. The Eight of Hearts in your deck should be the 10th card from the top of the deck.

To perform, tell a spectator that you will persuade him or her to choose a card according to the laws of numerology, but that the numbers will be of his or her own choosing. Hand over the deck and ask for a number between 10 and 20. (The trick won't work with 20!) Let's assume the pick is 16. Tell the spectator to deal 16 cards on to the table.

"Now put the rest of the deck aside and add the numbers of your chosen number," you say.

The number was 16; $1 + 6 = 7$. Tell the spectator to pick up the 16 cards and count down to the seventh. This card should be turned face up. The card in the envelope will be identical to the one chosen by the spectator.

KEY CARDS

ALL THE TRICKS IN THIS SECTION USE THE "KEY CARD"

PRINCIPLE. THE KEY CARD IS A CARD THAT IS KNOWN

TO THE PERFORMER AND LIES AT A CERTAIN POSITION

IN THE DECK. SOMETIMES IT IS MARKED,

SOMETIMES NOT. IN THE INTERESTS OF VARIETY,

SEVERAL DIFFERENT KEY CARDS WILL

BE DESCRIBED.

THE BUCKLE

The Effect

You find a selected card while holding the deck behind your back.

The Method

Spread out the deck, face down, and ask for a card to be chosen. As the spectator looks at the card, close the deck and bend it upwards (**Fig. 1**).

1

Spread the cards again and let the spectator put the card back anywhere in the spread. Hand the deck to the spectator for shuffling.

The chosen card is now the only flat card, which means the deck is markedly divided at the place where the card is inserted; the card automatically becomes the key (**Fig. 2**).

Take back the cards and square them. You will be able to see the break. If the chosen card is close to the top or bottom of the deck, make a cut to put it nearer the center. If the card is right on the top or bottom of the deck, leave it where it is.

2

other (**Fig 3**). Now gently cut the cards and you will feel them break naturally. The chosen card, which is now wider than the others, will be the bottom card of the upper part of the cut. Slide it out into your right hand (**Fig. 4**) and put the rest of the cards in your left hand.

Smile as you bring out the deck and put it down.

Widen your smile as you bring forward the chosen card and put it face up on the table.

Put the cards behind your back, saying you will find the selected card by feeling its vibrations.

With the deck behind your back, hold the cards lightly with the right thumb on one long edge and the right fingers on the

4

3

KEEP THINKING

The Method

Invite a spectator to shuffle a deck of cards. Take back the cards and spread them face down. Ask the spectator to pick one and look at it. Square the deck.

Tell the spectator to put the card back. Lift off half the deck with your right hand, extending your left hand for the return of the card. As you do, glance at the bottom card in your right hand (**Fig. 1**). This is your key card.

As soon as the spectator's card is returned, drop the cards from your right hand on top of it. Hand the spectator the complete deck, telling him or her to shuffle it.

NOTE: As long as the cards are shuffled in the normal overhand fashion, the key card and the chosen card will stay together, no matter how much the deck is shuffled and cut.

"Keep thinking Three of Diamonds, Three of Diamonds, Three of Diamonds . . . ," until the spectator realizes you are staring at him or her.

Then, you say "Your chosen card is the Three of Diamonds."

And, of course, it is.

Take back the deck and turn it face up. Start running the cards between your hands, looking for the key card (**Fig. 2**).

As you do this, tell the spectator to keep thinking of his or her card. "Keep thinking," you say, "Keep thinking . . . ."

As soon as you see the key card, you know the card on its right is the chosen card (**Fig. 3**). "Keep thinking," you murmur. Go past the chosen card, still murmuring.

CUTTING CORNERS

The Method

To make the key card, shorten the upper left and lower right corners of a face-down card with nail clippers or a pair of scissors (**Fig. 1**).

Now put the card in the deck. No matter which way the face-down cards are turned, the key card will have a short corner at the outer left corner of the deck.

left corner (**Fig. 2**); as the key card passes, you will hear—and feel—a click, caused by the short card and the card above it passing as one.

To stop at the key card, run your thumb once down the cards to get a rough idea where the key

To learn the technique of using this card, bury it in the deck and run your thumb down the outer positioned on top of the chosen card.) Now ask another spectator to shuffle the cards.

Finally, take back the deck and riffle to locate the key card. Give the deck a complete cut at that point. The key goes to the bottom and the chosen card is on top (**Fig. 4**).

Ask the spectator to name the chosen card, then drop the top card face up on the table as you say, "You can cut and shuffle all you like, but I always find the card I'm looking for."

card is located, then do it again, trying to stop at the exact spot. This will happen automatically as you gain experience—this technique is called "riffling."

To use the key, have it on the bottom of the deck as you spread the cards and ask for one card to be taken (**Fig. 3**). Put the deck on the table, tell the spectator to return the chosen card to the top, then ask him or her to cut the deck as many times as they wish. (The first cut ensures that the key is

MOVING FINGER

The Effect

A spectator makes you find his card—even though he or she has no idea where it is.

The Method

Your key is the top card of the deck. It is not marked, but on its back you have marked diagonally opposite corners with a pencil dot (**Fig. 1**).

1

Ask for a card to be selected, then cut the deck with your right hand. Offer the lower half for the return of the card.

The cards in your right hand are turned over ready for an overhand shuffle, and the key card (top) is drawn onto the lower pile (**Figs. 2 and 3**). Continue to shuffle the other cards on top. This looks perfectly fair, but of course the key card is now on top of the chosen card. When you have shuffled all the cards, give the deck a couple of cuts, then spread it face down in a ribbon across the table, noting the position of the key card.

2

3

You know the card with the dot (the key) is on the right of the chosen card. When you are almost above the key, start to bring your hand down. To the audience, your hand is being guided.

Let your finger come to rest on the card to the left of the key. Slide it out with your fingertips.

"Name your card," you say.

The spectator names it. Turn over the card. You have performed a miracle.

Ask the spectator to hold your wrist, then extend your arm over the cards at a height of about 20 inches, your finger pointing down (**Fig. 4**).

"You don't know where your card is," you say. "Neither do I. But concentrate on its name." Begin above one end of the ribbon and let the spectator draw your hand slowly along.

4

BLIND FAITH

The Method

The key card in this trick is a wide card, made by gluing together two cards slightly out of register so that the finished product is a card a fraction wider (and longer) than the others in the deck. Wherever this card lies in the deck, it can be easily located by touch. More importantly, it can also be used to mark the point at which the deck will be cut.

Have the key on the bottom as you spread the cards. Ask for one to be chosen. Tell the spectator to put his or her selection back on top. Make a complete cut, putting the key on top of the chosen card. Ask the spectator to shuffle the deck. Take back the deck and square it. You will be able to feel the key card. If it is near the top or bottom, make a couple of cuts openly. The idea is to get the card near the middle, where it is easier to cut. Put the deck on the table. Say, "You've done all you can to

lose that card of yours. But I have total faith in my ability to find it."

Without looking, cut it at the wide card, leaving the chosen card on top of the deck. Ask for the name of the chosen card. Still without looking, turn over the top card and throw it down, face up.

STACKED DECK

THE TRICKS IN THIS SECTION USE A STACKED DECK,

WHICH IS A DECK OF CARDS ARRANGED SO THAT YOU CAN

PERFORM ASTONISHING CARD TRICKS VERY EASILY.

THE STACK USED HERE IS THE ONE DEVISED BY

SI STEBBINS AND IS EXPLAINED AT THE

BEGINNING OF THE FIRST TRICK.

BLINDFOLD MIND PROBE

The Effect

You are blindfolded. A card is selected as usual. Without asking any questions, you correctly name the card.

The Method

Arrange the cards so they run in the order Ace, Four, Seven, Ten, King, Three, Six, Nine, Queen, Two, Five, Eight, Jack, and in the repeating order of Clubs, Hearts, Spades, Diamonds (**Fig. 1**).

1

Each card is three higher than the one before—e.g., if you cut a Two, the card beneath it will be a Five; cut a Nine and the next card will be 12 (a Queen). The suit order—Clubs, Hearts, Spades, Diamonds—is remembered by picturing the word CHaSeD. If you cut the Three of Hearts, the next card is the Six of Spades.

To perform the trick blindfolded, have the stacked deck ready in your hands; it can be cut as often as you wish without disturbing the stack. Ask a spectator to blindfold you with a large handkerchief, which you adjust "for comfort" with your thumbs, so you can see clearly down either side of your nose.

Spread the cards face down between your hands and ask for one to be chosen (**Fig. 2**). As it is taken, cut the deck at that point and put the bottom portion on top. Turn the deck face up for a moment as you square it and you will see the bottom card (**Fig. 3**)—let's say it's the Seven of Clubs.

Put down the cards. Ask the spectator to concentrate on his or her card.

The bottom card in the deck was originally above the selected card; it's a Seven, so the chosen card must be a 10—and it is a Club, so the chosen card must be a Heart—the 10 of Hearts.

"I'm getting an impression," you say, as soon as you have made the calculation. Slowly name the card.

THOUGHT PROCESS

The Effect

You predict two spectators' cards before they themselves know what cards they have chosen.

The Method

You will need two stacked decks. Put one deck in front of one spectator; hand the second deck to another spectator and tell him or her, "Hold the cards behind you."

Address the first spectator. "Cut that deck as many times as you want, complete cuts, putting the top half underneath each time." When that is done, say, "Take off the top card, don't look at it, and put it in your pocket. Now take the next card, no looking, and sit on it. Put the deck on the table."

Turn to the second spectator. "Cut the deck behind your back, then take off the top card, turn it face up, and slip it into the middle of the face-down deck." (**Fig. 1**)

Turn to the first spectator again. "I'm going to repeat your actions," you say, "and try to make my thought process recover the image of what you did."

Jack of Clubs," (the card after the Eight of Diamonds). Ask the first spectator to reveal the card he or she sat on. Again, a match! Turn to the second spectator and say, "Put the deck face up on the table."

Pick up the deck and glimpse the bottom card (e.g. the Five of Spades) (**Fig. 2**). Now mime the action of taking a card from the top and pocketing it then taking a second card and sitting on it.

"Now I'll look," you say. Take the invisible card from your pocket and name it: "The Eight of Diamonds" (the card after the Five of Spades). Ask the spectator to remove the card from his or her pocket. It matches!

Go through the same maneuver with the invisible card you sat on; stare at it, then say, "The

He or she does this (**Fig. 3**). You see which card is on top of the deck (e.g. the Ace of Clubs). You do a quick calculation, then announce, "The card you reversed in the deck is the Four of Hearts."

Spread the deck, find the face-down card, and turn it over—the Four of Hearts. You are a legend.

INTERLOPER

The Effect

While you are out of the room, a card is freely chosen from the deck, then put back. You return, look through the cards, and name the one that was chosen.

The Method

The deck is stacked. Ask a spectator to cut it as many times as he or she likes. When this has been done, square it up and put it in the middle of the table.

"I'm leaving the room," you say. "While I'm out, I want you to reach into the deck and take out a card. Show it to everyone, then put it back on top and cut it into the deck. When you've done that, call me in again." When you return to the room, pick up the cards and turn them face up. Spread them between your hands (**Fig. 1**), saying, "In the last couple of minutes, one card of these fifty-two has suffered a little more disturbance than the others.

removed, because there will simply be a gap in the sequence (**Fig. 2**).

The place where the card is inserted, however, will have a card that is out of sequence (**Fig. 3**). (In the picture, the odd card is the Seven of Hearts.)

When you find the card, pull it out.

I should be able to sense its stress as it passes through my fingers."

"I was right," you say. "This is a very badly stressed card." Turn it around and show its face. "Poor thing."

Start to go through the cards, taking your time. You note only the suits. The sequence of Clubs, Hearts, Spades, Diamonds is repeated over and over, all the way through the deck, except at the place where a card was removed, and at the place where it was replaced.

You will know where it was

SUPER SPELLER

The Effect

This trick appears to be a self-fulfilling prophecy. The look-alike of a chosen card is found by spelling out seven words.

The Method

Spread the stacked cards between your hands to have one chosen. Make the spread wide, emphasizing the freedom of choice (**Fig. 1**).

When the card is taken, break the deck at that point and put the cards from underneath on top. Now address the spectator.

"You took that card for me—that is my card. I want you to look at it and picture its look-alike. What I mean is, if you picked the Ace of Hearts, its look-alike would be the Ace of Diamonds, because it has the same color and the same number. The look-alike is your card."

Make sure that is clear, then continue. "I don't know what card you picked, neither does anybody else. Put it face down on the table in front of you, and keep thinking have just spoken (26 letters), putting down a card for each letter (**Fig. 2**). When you have put down the card for the last letter of "card," pause as you did when you spoke the phrase, then spell out the word "easily."

On the final letter, hold the card face down (**Fig. 3**). Tell the spectator to turn over the card on the table. Now reveal the one you hold. It is the look-alike—the spectator's card.

of its look-alike—your card." Pick up the deck and glimpse the bottom card—say the Six of Hearts. That means the spectator has the Nine of Spades. Believe it or not, the look-alike of this card, which is the Nine of Clubs, is halfway down the deck, at number 26 from the top.

"Now I will find your card," you say. Pause, then add, "easily."

Start to spell the words you

GROUP REVELATION

The Effect

Freely chosen cards are distributed among spectators. One by one, you reveal each of their selections.

The Method

The stacked deck is spread face down as you approach a spectator. "Pull out a bunch of cards," you say. "Keep one for yourself and hand out the rest to other spectators."

When the cards have been removed, cut the deck at that point, putting the lower part on top. Square the cards, glimpsing the bottom card. Let's say the spectator took six cards, and the card you glimpsed was the King of Diamonds. Now pretend you are gaining an impression of a dark card. Of course you start with the card that would have followed the King of Diamonds—the Three of Clubs. Name the card and ask if anyone has it. When it is returned, put it at the bottom of the deck.

Do the same with each successive card you reveal. As you proceed with the revelations, you will find that each spectator reacts, however slightly, when you name his or her card. Use these clues to home in on individuals. This will reinforce the idea that you're receiving "spirit" messages!

CLASSIC
TRICKS

CERTAIN CARD TRICKS HAVE AN IMPACT THAT SPECTATORS

REMEMBER LONG AFTER THE PERFORMANCE.

HERE ARE FIVE SUCH EFFECTS, ALL OF THEM TRIED AND

TRUE CLASSICS, ADAPTED TO BE EASILY PERFORMED

WITH MINIMAL PREPARATION.

SURPRISE ACES

The Effect

A trick appears to go wrong, then it goes right, and then there's an unexpected four-Ace finish. Tricks with Aces are always popular, which is why there are two in this section!

The Method

In this stack, the Aces are at the bottom; on top of them is a face-up Five. This setup enables easy overhand shuffling. The bottom five cards must not be disturbed.

1

To perform the trick, spread the face-down deck between your

hands, making sure the lower cards are bunched to hide the fact that one is face up (**Fig. 1**). Ask a spectator to select a card and remember it. Square the deck and put it on the table.

Ask the spectator to put the chosen card on top of the deck, then to lose it by cutting the deck and completing the cut. The chosen card will now be somewhere near the center of the deck, directly under the stack of four Aces.

2

Spread the deck in a ribbon across the table and smile confidently as you point to the face-up card (**Fig. 2**). The spectator will not hesitate to say that isn't his or her card.

"I know," you say, pushing out the card from the spread. "But this card tells me where your card is." Now count to five, pushing out a card for each number (the four Aces, plus one) (**Fig. 3**). Ask for the name of the spectator's selection and turn over the fifth card. It's the

spectator's card. "So I found it after all," you say.

Turn over the four Aces one by one. "And it seems that's not all I've found."

3

CUTTING THE ACES

The Effect

Magicians often demonstrate their skill by cutting the Aces; in this version, a spectator copies this without knowing how it was done!

The Method

A fresh deck of cards is prepared by putting the four Aces on top of the deck. The trick is to keep your eye on the pile with the four Aces on top.

Put the cards on the table and ask a spectator to cut them into four roughly equal piles (**Fig. 1**). Say, "I want you to mix the top cards in the following way." Point at a pile (not the one with the Aces), tell the spectator to pick it up, transfer three cards from the top to the bottom of the pile, then put one card on the top of each of the three piles on the table (**Fig. 2**). The spectator must now put down the stack he or she is holding and repeat fourth pile is back on the table, ask if the spectator knows what has happened. The answer will probably be "no."

"Well," you say, "if my guess is correct, it's something pretty spectacular . . . ." Turn over the top cards one by one (**Fig. 3**), and show how clever spectators can be when they do as they're told.

the actions with the other three piles. Point to the piles in turn, being careful to point last to the pile with the four Aces.

By the time the fourth pile is picked up, the procedure of transferring cards from other piles will have put three extra cards on top of the Aces. These will go to the bottom of the pile when the Ace pile is picked up and the transferring is carried out for the last time. When the

SENSE OF TOUCH

The Effect

The performer finds a selected card using only his or her sense of touch.

The Method

The cards are shuffled and a spectator is asked to think of a number between one and 20. The spectator memorizes the card that lies at his or her chosen number from the top of the deck.

Now take the deck from him or her and say this: "Only you know the number and the card. Even so, I can find the card by sense of touch alone."

Put the deck behind your back. Take off the bottom card and put it on top of the deck. Peel off the new bottom card and bring it forward, back facing out.

"I think I have found your card," you say, and slip it into your pocket.

Bring the deck forward again. "If I'm wrong, then your card will still be at your number. What's the number?"

Suppose it's 10. Count cards off the top of the deck one at a time, face down. When you come to the 10th card, slide it across the table.

"If I'm wrong, that's your card."

The next stage is not sleight of hand, but a straightforward move. As the spectator reaches for the card on the table, you lift the inner end of the next card (his or her chosen card!) with your thumb and let it drop back against your curled pinkie, which now pushes the card into the curl of your opposite hand (**Figs. 1 and 2**), where it stays (**Fig. 3**).

The spectator turns over the card. It's not the "right" one. While this is happening, slip your hand into your pocket. Slide the card from your palm to your fingertips and bring it out. Ask the name of the spectator's card. Show that you were right.

COUNTDOWN

The Effect

Although the performer never touches the cards, he or she knows exactly where a chosen card lies in the deck.

The Method

From bottom to top, stack the Ace to Ten of any one suit (e.g. Diamonds) (**Fig. 1**). The cards are in this position when you put the deck, face down, in front of a spectator.

"From now on," you say, "I'm not going to touch the cards. I want you to spread the deck and slide out one card, then square up the deck again."

Now tell the spectator to look at the card removed from the deck.

"Put it back on top and give the deck a full cut, which will bury the card."

When the card is buried, tell the spectator to turn the deck face up, rest a fingertip on the top card for a second (**Fig. 2**), then give the deck another complete cut. What happens next will depend on how the deck is cut. As soon as the top card is a Diamond with a value anywhere between Ace and Ten, you know where the chosen card lies. For example, if the spectator cuts the Four of Diamonds to the top of the deck, then the chosen card will be at position number four when the deck is face down. If no Diamond card shows, ask the spectator to press a finger on the top card again (a red herring!) and cut once more. As soon as a Diamond between Ace and Ten

shows, remember it—let's say it's the Three (**Fig. 3**). Tell the spectator to turn the deck face down.

"Put a finger on the deck again and think of your card," you say. "I sense its position . . . . It's at number five from the top. Whoops! You moved! Now it's at number four . . . no, you moved again. Now it's at number three. Take a look. Quick, before it moves again!"

The spectator counts to number three (or whatever) and there, sure enough, is the chosen card (**Fig. 4**).

INSTANT SPELL

The Effect

A spectator finds his or her own chosen card by spelling its name. Of all the methods of achieving this classic effect, this is the most direct.

The Method

Put the 10 of Clubs, Six of Spades, Jack of Hearts, Eight of Spades, and Nine and Queen of Diamonds face down on the deck, then nine assorted cards on top.

Start moving cards from your left hand to your right, without reversing their order. As you reach the fifth or sixth card, say, "Stop me when you like." Speak a little impatiently—you will almost certainly be stopped on one of the set-up cards. (If you are not stopped, change tactics; spot the bottom card of the deck and perform a "key card" trick!)

Show the spectator the card he or she stopped at, and say, "Look at this card and remember it." Put

the card back on the deck and drop all the right-hand cards on top of it. The deck is now as it was at the start. Hand the cards to the spectator and say, "Spell out the name of your card, starting from the top of the deck, including the word 'of.'" The spectator's card will show up on the final letter "S."